D1170908

Hard to Crack
Nut Trees

Meredith Sayles Hughes

Lerner Publications Company/Minneapolis

Lerner Publications Company
A division of Lerner Publishing Group
241 First Avenue North
Minneapolis, MN 55401 U.S.A.

Website address: www.lernerbooks.com

Designers: Edward Mack and Jessie Lohman
Editors: Katy Holmgren, Heather Hooper
Photo Researcher: Kirsten Frickle

Check out the author's website at www.foodmuseum.com

3 9082 10711 1851

LIBRARY OF CONGRESS CATALOGING-IN-
PUBLICATION DATA

Hughes, Meredith Sayles.
    Hard to crack: nut trees / by Meredith Sayles Hughes
        p. cm. — (Plants we eat)
    Includes index.
    Summary: Presents information on the history,
growing requirements, uses, and food value of various
nuts grown around the world. Includes recipes.
    ISBN 0-8225-2838-X (lib. bdg. : alk. paper)
    1. Nuts—United States Juvenile literature. 2. Nut
Trees—United States Juvenile literature. 3. Cookery
(Nuts) [1. Nuts. 2. Nut trees. 3. Cookery—Nuts.]
I. Title. II. Title: Nut trees. III. Series: Hughes,
Meredith Sayles. Plants we eat.
SB401.A45U555 2001
641.3'45—dc21   99-32071

Manufactured in the United States of America
1 2 3 4 5 6 – JR – 06 05 04 03 02 01

The glossary on page 85 gives definitions of
words shown in **bold type** in the text.

Contents

Introduction

Plants make all life on our planet possible. They provide the oxygen we breathe and the food we eat. Think about a burger and fries. The meat comes from cattle, which eat plants. The fries are potatoes cooked in oil from soybeans, corn, or sunflowers. The burger bun is a wheat product. Ketchup is a mixture of tomatoes, herbs, and corn syrup or the sugar from sugarcane. How about some onions or pickle relish with your burger?

How Plants Make Food

By snatching sunlight, water, and carbon dioxide from the atmosphere and mixing them together—a complex process called **photosynthesis**—green plants create food energy. The raw food energy is called glucose, a simple form of sugar. From this storehouse of glucose, each plant produces fats, carbohydrates, and proteins—the elements that make up the bulk of the foods humans and animals eat.

Sunlight peeks through the branches of a plant-covered tree in a tropical rain forest, where all the elements exist for photosynthesis to take place.

First we eat, then we do everything else.

—M. F. K. Fisher

Plants offer more than just food. They provide the raw materials for making the clothes you're wearing and the paper in books, magazines, and newspapers. Much of what's in your home comes from plants—the furniture, the wallpaper, and even the glue that holds the paper on the wall. Eons ago plants created the gas and oil we put in our cars, buses, and airplanes. Plants even give us the gum we chew.

On the Move

Although we don't think of plants as beings on the move, they have always been pioneers. From their beginnings as algaelike creatures in the sea to their movement onto dry land about 400 million years ago, plants have colonized new territories. Alone on the barren rock of the earliest earth, plants slowly established an environment so rich with food, shelter, and oxygen that some forms of marine life took up residence on dry land. Helped along by birds who scattered seeds far and wide, plants later sped up their travels, moving to cover most of our planet.

Early in human history, when few people lived on the earth, gathering food was everyone's main activity. Small family groups were nomadic, venturing into areas that offered a source of water, shelter, and foods such as fruits, nuts, seeds, and small game animals. After they had eaten up the region's food sources, the family group moved on to another spot. Only when people noticed that food plants were renewable—that berry bushes would bear fruit again and that grasses gave forth seeds year after year—did family groups begin to settle in any one area for more than a single season.

Organisms that behave like algae—small, rootless plants that live in water

It's a Fact!

The term *photosynthesis* comes from Greek words meaning "putting together with light." This chemical process, which takes place in a plant's leaves, is part of the natural cycle that balances the earth's store of carbon dioxide and oxygen.

Native Americans were the first peoples to plant crops in the Americas.

time on their hands, so they turned to refining their skills at making tools and shelter and to developing writing, pottery, and other crafts.

Plants We Eat

This series examines the wide range of plants people around the world have chosen to eat. You will discover where plants came from, how they were first grown, how they traveled from their original homes, and where they have become important and why. Along the way, each book looks at the impact of certain plants on society and discusses the ways in which these food plants are sown, harvested, processed, and sold. You will also discover that some plants are key characters in exciting high-tech stories. And there are plenty of opportunities to test recipes and to dig into other hands-on activities.

Domestication of plants probably began as an accident. Seeds from a wild plant eaten at dinner were tossed onto a trash pile. Later a plant grew there, was eaten, and its seeds were tossed onto the pile. The cycle continued on its own until someone noticed the pattern and repeated it deliberately. Agriculture radically changed human life. From relatively small plots of land, more people could be fed over time, and fewer people were required to hunt and gather food. Diets shifted from a broad range of wild foods to a more limited but more consistent menu built around one main crop, such as wheat, corn, cassava, rice, or potatoes. With a stable food supply, the world's population increased and communities grew larger. People had more

The series Plants We Eat divides food plants into a variety of informal categories. Some plants are prized for their seeds, others for their fruits, and some for their underground roots, tubers, or bulbs. Many plants offer leaves or stalks for good eating. Humans convert some plants into oils and others into beverages or flavorings. In *Hard to Crack: Nut Trees*, we'll look at one of the oldest portable foods on earth, the nut. A nut is a firm, usually crunchy **kernel** found inside a shell. The word *nut* can also refer to the entire object, from the fleshy outside to the inner shell and kernel. While there are hundreds of nuts throughout the world, this book will focus on pecans, walnuts, macadamias, almonds, pistachios, and cashews.

Nuts share common characteristics. All nuts grow on trees and are nutritionally similar. They're packed with useful oil and protein. They provide fiber and energy-giving fat. Most nuts develop from flowers. A shell surrounds the kernel of each nut. But not all shells are the same—the almond's is soft compared to the macadamia's. A fibrous husk covers the shells of the macadamia, pistachio, and pecan. Both husk and fleshy fruit cover walnut and almond shells.

Thousands of years before 10,000 B.C—when people began growing their own food—humans visited groves of nut trees. An abundant food, nuts are simple to gather and store. They require no cooking or processing beyond shelling. Unlike meat, nuts keep well for months, so ancient people relied on stored nuts in times of scarcity, such as drought.

Nuts are no longer a **staple food** for most people. But nuts are still vital to the agricultural economy of many areas. These days, edible nuts are eaten as nutritious snacks, are put on top of baked goods, or are used to flavor sauces.

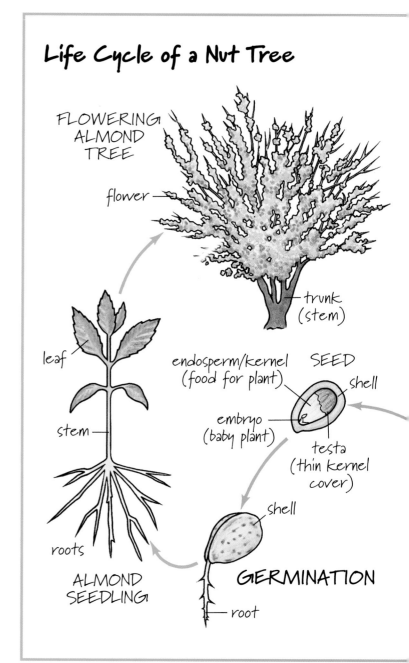

Life Cycle of a Nut Tree

FLOWERING ALMOND TREE

flower

trunk (stem)

leaf

stem

roots

ALMOND SEEDLING

endosperm/kernel (food for plant)

SEED

shell

embryo (baby plant)

testa (thin kernel cover)

shell

GERMINATION

root

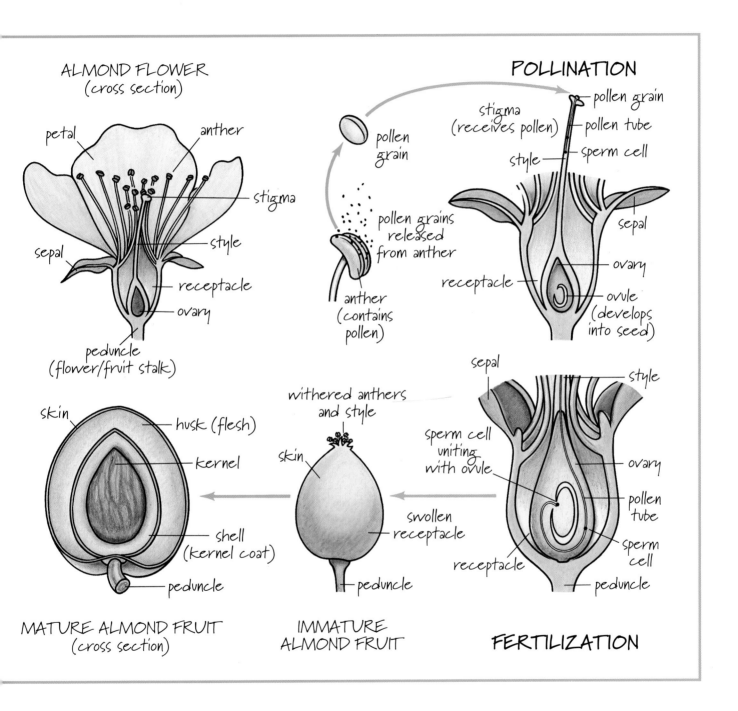

ALMOND FLOWER
(cross section)

petal

anther

stigma

style

receptacle

ovary

sepal

peduncle
(flower/fruit stalk)

POLLINATION

pollen
grain

stigma
(receives pollen)

pollen grain

pollen tube

sperm cell

style

sepal

pollen grains
released
from anther

anther
(contains
pollen)

receptacle

ovary

ovule
(develops
into seed)

skin

husk (flesh)

kernel

shell
(kernel coat)

peduncle

MATURE ALMOND FRUIT
(cross section)

withered anthers
and style

skin

swollen
receptacle

peduncle

IMMATURE
ALMOND FRUIT

sepal

style

sperm cell
uniting
with ovule

ovary

pollen
tube

sperm
cell

receptacle

peduncle

FERTILIZATION

Pecans

[*Carya illinoensis*]

The pecan has a lot to brag about—it's one of the few native North American nuts to thrive as a major agricultural crop. The pecan sprang from North America's south-central region, a large area including thirteen states and part of northern Mexico. The towering pecan tree grows wild in many parts of Texas, where it is prized for its hardwood and as a shade tree. Pecan trees can live to be well over one hundred years old.

The pecan tree grows over 150 feet high and produces slim, toothy, bright green leaves. A deciduous (leaf-shedding) tree, the pecan bursts with both male and female flowers in spring. The male flowers hang down in exuberant furry clusters. The female flowers develop into nuts, which also grow in clusters. Their long, glossy shells of bright pink and rich brown hide thin husks. When cracked open, the sweet, moist kernel divides into halves.

The pecan tree thrives in the southern United States.

I wish I had a dollar for every pecan I've eaten. I'd be richer than Rockefeller.

—A hostess in Natchez, Mississippi

Spanish explorer Hernando de Soto

The pecan and the walnut are members of the huge botanical family known as Juglans. The family includes all the world's hickories and walnuts. Both nuts have hard shells, which protect tasty kernels that look something like a human brain.

Pecan Origins

The first pecan tree probably appeared in the Mississippi and Ohio River Valleys of what would become Illinois and Missouri. During the last Ice Age, the Gulf of Mexico reached as far north as the mouth of the Ohio River.

As the gulf shrank, pecan seeds may have washed down the Ohio. The seeds may have lodged in rich soils left behind by the gulf water in Arkansas, Louisiana, Oklahoma, and along the coasts of Texas and Mexico.

Along the southern part of the Mississippi River Valley, North Americans began to harvest wild pecans at least eight thousand years ago. They ate the pecan—a staple food—roasted, ground into meal, and mixed with fruits and beans. They mixed corn and boiled pecans to make cakes. Fermented (alcoholic) pecan flour became a powerful drink called *powcohicoria,* used in the ceremonies of Algonquian-speaking people.

Scholars believe that the Choctaw, who were then settled between the Mississippi and Alabama Rivers, were the first to cultivate the pecan. Their efforts and methods influenced other people living in the Mississippi Valley to follow suit. When Europeans arrived in the area during the 1500s, Native Americans found pecans to be a valuable trade good. They traded the nuts with newcomers for European goods.

A Spanish expedition in 1533 explored south-central Texas along the Guadalupe River, north of what would become San Antonio. A member of the group, Lope de Oviedo, described the abundance of pecans.

He wrote, "There were many nuts on the banks of this river which the Indians ate in their season, coming from twenty to thirty leagues about." The Guadalupe River was known to Native Americans of eastern Texas's Galveston Island as "the river of nuts," or pecans.

Spaniard Hernando de Soto, who led the first group of European explorers to spot the Mississippi River, found pecan trees in what became Alabama. In 1541 a member of his party wrote that pecans, mulberries, and plums were important parts of the local Choctaw Indians' diet.

French trappers and traders in North America also enjoyed pecans. European chroniclers described these American nuts as

Family Matters

To keep things straight in the huge families of plants and animals, scientists classify and name living things by grouping them according to shared features. These various characteristics become more noticeable in each of seven major categories. The categories are kingdom, division or phylum, class, order, family, genus, and species. Species share the most features in common, while members of a kingdom or division share far fewer traits. This system of scientific classification and naming is called taxonomy. Scientists refer to plants and animals by a two-part Latin or Greek term made up of the genus and the species name. The genus name comes first, followed by the species name. Look at the pecan's taxonomic name on page 10. Can you figure out to what genus the pecan belongs? And to what species?

The Pine Nut

Pine trees aren't just valuable as Christmas trees and lumber. A dozen members of the species produce tasty, slender pine nuts. In North Africa, Spain, Portugal, and Italy, the Italian stone pine produces the *pignoli*. The Swiss stone pine grows in the Alps. A wild pine called the *piñon* thrives in the American Southwest. Other pine trees in northern Mexico produce nuts. Asia boasts four different varieties of pine nuts. The Chinese pine nut is often a cheaper buy in North American supermarkets than are piñon nuts.

The pine nut has a long history. Ancient Greeks coated it in honey. Roman soldiers carried the nuts as far as Great Britain, where archaeologists have unearthed the shells. In North America, people gathered piñon nuts by hand more than six thousand years ago. They nibbled them right from the shell, but they cooked the tasty nut as well. People roasted and ground the pine nuts into meal that could be made into paste or mixed in soup. Many people use similar methods in modern times. Cooks blend cheese, basil, and pignoli to make pesto, the uncooked summertime sauce that is perfect on pasta. If you're a pine nut fan who wants to raise some of the tasty nuts, be prepared to be patient. The North American pine doesn't produce any nuts for its first twenty-five years and only reaches its peak at age seventy-five.

"a kind of very small walnut." Traders began carrying the nuts from the Illinois region to the British colonies along the American Atlantic coast around 1760. Buyers called the pecans "Illinois nuts."

A Cultivated Nut

Pecans came into their own as a southern specialty when a planter named Le Page du Pratz wrote *The History of Louisiana* in 1763.

(Many years later, President Thomas Jefferson read du Pratz's book to learn about the area before making the Louisiana Purchase.) Du Pratz praised Louisiana's pralines. The sweet patty was traditionally made in France by cooks using caramelized sugar and almonds. In Louisiana, pecans stood in for almonds, and brown sugar took the place of white. In modern times, pralines are still popular across the United States.

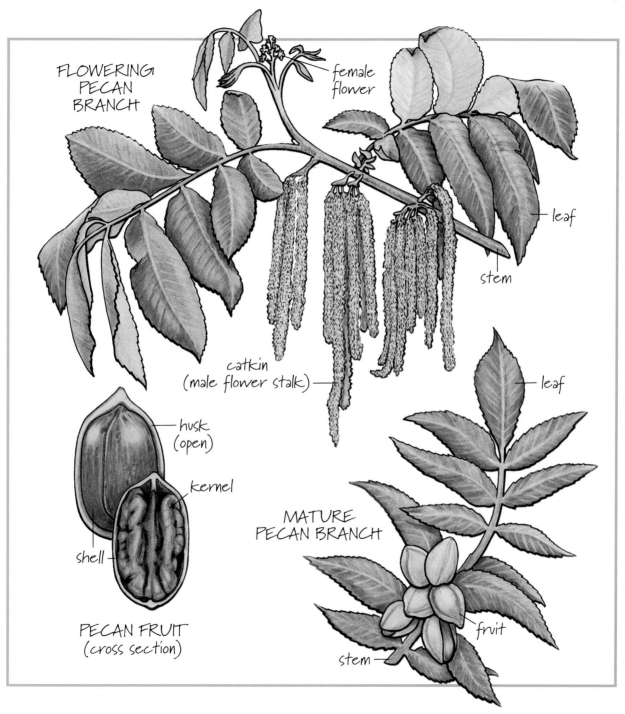

FLOWERING
PECAN
BRANCH

female
flower

leaf

stem

catkin
(male flower stalk)

leaf

husk
(open)

kernel

shell

MATURE
PECAN BRANCH

PECAN FRUIT
(cross section)

fruit

stem

The Nutcracker

Over time people have developed all manner of nutcracker to crack the shells of tough nuts. The finest designs open the shell without crushing the kernel inside. Perhaps the most famous nutcracker is the one that comes alive in E.T.A. Hoffman's 1816 fairy tale. Peter Tchaikovsky, the Russian composer, set the tale to music in his famous ballet *The Nutcracker* in 1892.

The gardens at Monticello

A couple of George Washington's majestic pecan trees still stand at Mount Vernon.

By 1772 a New York nurseryman named William Prince was raising pecan trees from nuts he planted. He sold a few of the ten trees that grew to customers in England. We have no word as to how well they grew so far beyond the pecan's usual home.

George Washington raised pecan trees at Mount Vernon, his Virginia home, in 1775. And according to the brother of French botanist Du Mont de Courset, Washington carried pecans in his pocket to snack on during the Revolutionary War.

Thomas Jefferson obtained what he called "paccan nuts" from the Mississippi Valley. His slaves planted pecan trees and the nuts at Monticello, his Virginia home, around the year 1780. Jefferson enjoyed the beauty of his pecan trees. But even after twenty years, the trees had not borne fruit. He supposed that the trees' need for lots of water wasn't being met at Monticello. Other accounts indicate that hogs may have assaulted the pecan trees.

Grafting and Growing Pecans

In modern times, growers raise pecans in southern states from Georgia to Arizona. Georgia leads the nation's pecan production with about 105 million pounds from commercial **cultivars.** In New Mexico and Arizona, farmers raise pecans in huge irrigated orchards. Texas averages an annual pecan harvest of 70 million pounds. Seventy percent comes from one-hundred-year-old trees found along rivers in east and central Texas. Commercial farmers raise pecans in Mexico, Australia, Brazil, Israel, and South Africa. With the exception of Mexico, these countries' production figures remain low.

Nurseries raise most young pecan trees sold to farmers. Growers at the nurseries create most **cultivated** pecan trees by **grafting,** or joining parts of two trees to grow into a single tree. When a planter raises a pecan tree from seed, there's no certain way to know what the tree will be like. The trees will have inherited all sorts of characteristics from their pecan ancestors. So the tree might not be healthy or sturdy. The nuts might have a thick, hard-to-crack shell or a poor flavor. Of course, the tree could be perfectly healthy, live for a hundred years, and have terrific nuts. But because there's no way to tell, most growers prefer the safer growing method of grafting. Farmers choose a pecan tree with particularly desirable characteristics, then they graft a small part of that tree onto rootstock. This way farmers can have

When the pecan is ripe, the husk cracks open.

Horticulturists inspect a plant for signs of pecan scab damage, a fungus that attacks pecan trees during rainy weather.

an orchard of healthy, standard pecan trees that will bear enough nuts to sell for a profit.

Growers do raise some pecan trees from the seeds of varieties (types) chosen for their sturdiness. The seed-grown trees become rootstock, onto which growers graft scions (parts of another pecan tree with desirable characteristics, such as an especially flavorful nut). Over time, the rootstock and the scion grow together. The new, single pecan tree combines the qualities of the original trees. Growers have developed more than three hundred pecan varieties. The breeders work to create pecans with specific sizes, colors, weights, tastes, or special characteristics, such as resistance to disease or drought.

Stuart and Desirable are two famous pecan varieties. Others bear the names of Native American groups such as Choctaw, Cheyenne, and Caddo.

Growers can choose from several methods of grafting. A worker can insert one or two shoots of the scion under the bark of the sawed-off rootstock. Nursery workers cover this kind of graft with beeswax or tape to protect the operation from rain and insects. To use a different grafting technique, called "top working," orchard workers cut a mature pecan tree off at the top and attach scions to it.

A third method is known as "ring budding." Instead of a shoot, a worker inserts a small piece of bark containing a scion's bud (a place from which a new branch will grow) under the rootstock's bark. Growers wrap this with waxed cloth or tape for twelve to fifteen days. If the buds turn green or grow plump within this time, the graft is a success. The grower can safely remove the protective wax or tape.

When the young trees reach three years old and five or six feet tall, farmers plant the trees in orchards. Workers set the trees thirty to fifty feet apart. Because so much

The pecan tree is the tallest and fastest-growing tree of the hickory family.

space stretches between trees and because the trees take six or seven years to begin producing, many pecan growers **intercrop.** They plant vegetables, grapes, cotton, wheat, or even fruit-bearing trees between the pecan trees. In Georgia peach trees grow among pecan trees.

The typical pecan tree needs a little over fifty inches of water per year to thrive. Some varieties require more and some less. The trees require most of the water during their peak growing season of April to October. To ensure that the trees get enough water, many growers use systems such as drip irrigation (hoses on the ground) combined with sprayers. Six-inch-high sprayers deliver precise amounts of water to individual trees.

Harvesting the Pecan

At harvesttime in the fall, workers in small orchards may collect the nuts by hand. The nuts must be collected swiftly and efficiently because growers hope to get the nuts to market by December, the peak selling period for pecans.

Workers climb tall ladders to a tree's upper branches. Helpers hand ten-foot-long cedar poles to the workers, who thresh the tree by banging the branches until the nuts fall down. Sometimes people on the ground whack the branches with long plastic pipes. Others toss threshing sticks up into the tree to shake the nuts loose. Then workers

A food vendor sells pecans in Tlequepaque, a suburb of Guadalajara, Mexico.

through and around the nuts for up to seventeen hours. The drying prevents the nuts from getting moldy. The workers move plastic bins of pecans to a huge refrigerator or to a freezer. The choice depends on how long the produce will be stored before it is sold.

Years ago, people cracked their own pecans at home. In modern times, more than 85 percent of all pecans sold are shelled. Consumers want their nuts in convenient form. When the pecans are brought out from cold storage for shelling, they must be warmed in close-to-boiling water. This softens the shells and also kills bacteria. The nuts are then cracked forcefully on one end by a machine that can handle dozens of nuts at a time. The kernel is separated from the shell by a machine called a sheller. Next, moist kernels are dried and cooled down before packaging. Pecan halves and pieces end up in cellophane bags, shrink-wrapped packages, and glass or plastic jars.

Peckish for Pecans

Bakers of cookies, cakes, pies, and tea breads love this North American native. People make fancy candies and confections, such as pralines, butter pecan ice cream, pecan sandies, and pecan brittle. Some folks nibble fine nuts glazed with sugar or orange juice. Texans with a sweet tooth are satisfied by an array of pecan confections, such as date, pecan, and orange bread.

methodically collect the fallen pecans under and around the base of the tree. Some orchards open their acres to "pick it yourself" visitors who do the grower's labor. In return for the work, customers can buy freshly picked pecans less expensively than in stores.

Most large commercial enterprises use mechanical shakers. The long-armed machines grasp the tree in a bear hug and shake the nuts to the ground. An orchard worker uses a vacuum-cleaner-like harvester to pick up the fallen nuts, along with twigs and leaves. Other machines separate the pecans from the debris and then clean and sort the nuts.

Workers lay the pecans on racks in storage facilities, where large fans blow warm air

Dig In!

PRALINE PECAN DESSERT BARS
(MAKES EIGHTEEN BARS)

½ cup butter at room temperature
1⅛ cups flour
⅛ teaspoon salt
1 teaspoon white sugar
2 eggs
1 cup brown sugar
1 teaspoon baking powder
1 cup pecans

These delicious bars are the ultimate in sweet crunchy treats from Texas. Preheat the oven to 375°. In a medium-sized bowl, mix the butter, one cup of flour, salt, and white sugar until the blend is crumbly. Use your fingers to press the mixture into an eight-inch baking pan. Bake it for ten to fifteen minutes.

While the bars are baking, beat the eggs in a medium-sized bowl. Add the brown sugar, baking powder, and remaining flour. Mix well, add the pecans, and stir it until the pecans are well coated.

Carefully remove the pan from the oven. Spread the pecan mix over the bars. Be careful—the pan is still very hot. Return the pan to the oven for fifteen minutes. After you take the pan out, let the bars cool. Then slice them up and enjoy!

They snack on pecan cake, little nut tarts called tassies, and pecan-filled date cookies. Pecan pie is a favorite dessert in the southern United States. Each region guards its own secret pecan pie ingredients with a passion. According to our sources, one area adds maple syrup and another a dash of Kentucky bourbon.

But sweet desserts aren't the only way to use pecans. The nuts add flavor to bread-and-sausage stuffing for turkey, chicken, and wild game. Bakers make bread with finely ground pecans and no flour. Chicken gets a boost when the bird is dipped in a buttermilk and crushed pecan concoction before baking. And some nuts are roasted in butter, salted, and eaten by the pound.

Native also to northern Mexico, the pecan is popular with Mexican cooks. Ground pecans may be an ingredient in mole, a sauce made with chilies, tomatoes, tomatillos, and chocolate, among other ingredients. Pecan brittle and pecan pie are Mexican favorites, too.

Carbon Dating

The oldest known pecan seeds and leaves, found in Texas at Baker's Cave, are carbon-dated to between 6100–3000 B.C. Before carbon dating, archaeologists and others who studied the past had no reliable way of determining an artifact's exact age. The best they could do was make guesses based on how deep in the ground the object was and the kinds of things found nearby. In the late 1940s, an American chemist named Willard F. Libby discovered a more accurate way to date organic (carbon-based) matter.

All living things contain carbon. Plants absorb carbon from the atmosphere, and animals eat the plants or other animals. A tiny amount of this carbon is carbon 14, a radioactive form of carbon that breaks down at a steady rate.

When a plant or animal dies, it stops taking in carbon 14. Because scientists know how long it takes carbon 14 to decay, they can determine when the organism died by measuring the amount of carbon 14 the object contains.

Experts use carbon dating to learn the ages of bones, wood, pollen, seeds, and other artifacts. Even nonorganic artifacts like pottery and fabric, which contain some carbon, can be dated using this method.

Send a Nut to Space

Low in sodium and high in protein, pecans have their own unique claim to fame in the health arena. In the late 1960s, the National Aeronautics and Space Administration (NASA) looked for a nutritious snack for its moon-bound astronauts. The food item had to be full of energy, easy to digest, unaffected by extremes of temperature, and most important, delicious. Naturally NASA chose the pecan. The nuts were washed, fumigated, and fussed over before being vacuum-packed in extra thick polyethylene. Pecans went aloft with the crews of both Apollo 13 (1970) and Apollo 14 (1971). Of the two, only Apollo 14 landed on the moon. We suspect that during the thirty-three-and-a-half hours spent on the lunar surface, someone in the spacecraft must have popped a pecan.

In a Nutshell

Hard-as-a-rock pecan shells have a variety of uses. In areas of abundant pecans, gardeners use shells instead of bark to **mulch** (provide a protective covering for) plants. Crushed shells substitute for gravel on paths or driveways. Powdered shells remove grease from engines and are an ingredient in wood veneer and fertilizers. Pecan tree timber, a hardwood, is used for flooring and durable furniture.

It's a Fact!

Pecan means "nut too hard to crack by hand" in Algonquian, a language family spoken from eastern Canada to the Rocky Mountains. The word originally referred to a range of nuts, including wild hickories and black walnuts. Eventually the name singled out only the pecan.

A NASA scientist tests a pecan pie.

Walnuts
[*Juglans regia*]

The walnut is the oldest nut in the basket. The stately walnut tree boasts gray bark and elegant branches sporting small, pointed bright green leaves. Round, green fruit hides the wrinkled nutshell and the golden kernel. The Juglans family includes more than fifteen nuts native to Asia, Europe, and the Americas. The English or Persian walnut (*Juglans regia*) is the most important worldwide. North America's black walnut (*J. nigra*) has fans on a more limited scale.

The English walnut is the most widely grown walnut in the world.

He who plants a walnut tree expects not to eat of its fruit.

—English proverb

The Walnut's Saga

The ancient tree's exact origins remain unknown. But the nut probably sprang from southeastern Europe, the Middle East, and the mountains of northern India, where the walnut tree grew wild. Prehistoric people who traveled seasonally in search of food may have carried the nut tree to other parts of Europe and Asia. The oldest remains of wild walnuts have been dated to 50,000 B.C. Archaeologists found the nuts in Iraq's Shanidar caves, home to Neanderthals.

The domestication of the walnut probably began more than twelve thousand years ago, when ancient walnut lovers planted the best-tasting, thinnest-shelled nuts. Over many generations, varieties of cultivated walnuts

A man weighs walnuts at a bazaar in Srinigar, India.

The ancient Greeks bought walnuts at large outdoor markets like this one.

emerged. Thousands of years ago, herders carried these domesticated nuts east and west, spreading the walnut even farther. By 7000 B.C., early people living at the edges of lakes in Switzerland—a considerable distance from the nut's original home—were enjoying the walnut.

Familiar to people of the Middle East, walnuts are mentioned in the Old Testament of the Bible. The walnuts enjoyed in ancient Europe were obtained either by European visitors to Persia (what would become Iran) or by Persian traders journeying to Europe. Greece probably received the walnut somewhere between 550 B.C. and 350 B.C. and the Romans somewhat later. China had the walnut by 100 B.C.

The Roman scholar and naturalist Pliny the Elder considered the walnut tree too shady, depressing people and harming the growth of nearby plants. Nonetheless, Roman bridegrooms tossed walnuts at the wedding crowd. This symbolized fertility and the groom's commitment to maturity. Romans probably ate walnuts and fresh fruit as a dessert. Archaeologists discovered evidence of that custom while excavating the ruins of Pompeii, a Roman city buried in ash by a volcanic eruption in A.D. 79. An after-dinner portion of walnuts in the shell was found on a table at the Temple of Isis (an Egyptian nature goddess also worshiped by Romans). Researchers found almonds, chestnuts, filberts, and walnuts among the ruins.

Some scholars think the Romans spread the walnut throughout Europe. By about A.D. 150, the Roman Empire had spread across Europe, from Spain to Britain to the shores of the Black Sea, into the Anatolian Peninsula (Turkey), down the Mediterranean coast to Egypt, and all along the coast of North Africa. But evidence suggests that the Gauls, a Celtic tribe of what would become France, had the walnut well before the Roman invasion of 58 B.C. Either way, this is clearly a well-traveled nut. By the fourth century A.D., walnuts grew in France near the town of Grenoble, a walnut powerhouse even in modern times. By A.D. 800 Charlemagne, a Frankish king, ordered the planting of walnut trees. During this period, cooks used walnuts to flavor stew.

The volcanic eruption that buried Pompeii burned these nuts.

We Hate to Break It to You, but. . . .

The doughnut is not a nut. The snack started out as a ball of dough left over from making bread. For centuries, thrifty Dutch cooks boiled said ball in oil to make *olykoek*, or oily cake. As early as the 1600s, Americans dubbed the cakes "dough nuts." By the close of the 1700s, cooks poked holes in the ball of dough to speed up the cooking process.

To Your Health!

Polyunsaturated fats are essential fatty acids. These fats actually combat heart disease because they're vital parts of blood and body membranes. They also help to control the flow of blood and may help to lower blood cholesterol levels. Although mostly found in salmon or tuna fish oil, polyunsaturated fat also turns up in walnuts. And the walnut oil used on salads fights skin cancer.

Walnuts are rich in magnesium, a mineral that helps the body use calcium and potassium. Magnesium also aids the proper functioning of the nervous system.

Throughout Europe in the Middle Ages, people made and used walnut oil, which was particularly popular in France. Cooks pounded walnuts into a paste that thickened soups. The wealthy ate walnut sauces more than the poor, who had little with which to make a sauce and less on which to pour it. But for generations, tasty wild walnuts were a staple food of poor people. In times of famine, desperate people even ate the shells! Ground walnut shells mixed with liquid can make a kind of bread.

In the 1500s, walnuts were known in England. Walnuts didn't make much of an impact there, with one exception. Whole walnuts, greenish outer flesh and all, pickled in vinegar, became a British specialty.

A squirrel enjoys a walnut snack.

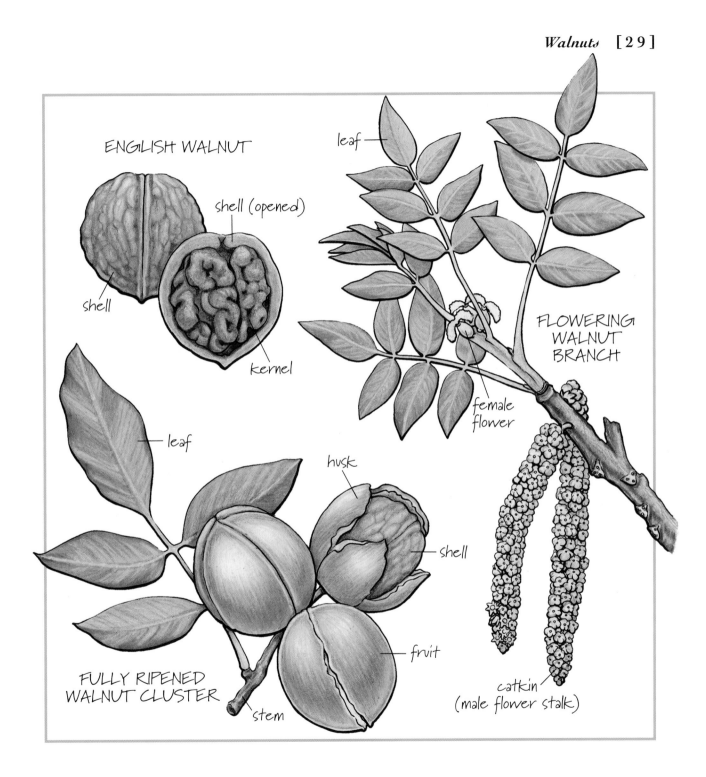

ENGLISH WALNUT

shell (opened)

shell

kernel

leaf

FLOWERING
WALNUT
BRANCH

female
flower

leaf

husk

shell

fruit

FULLY RIPENED
WALNUT CLUSTER

stem

catkin
(male flower stalk)

A painting from the Middle Ages shows a jester throwing nuts and goodies.

Beginning in the 1600s, seafaring English merchants carried walnuts across the globe. Brought to New England and Virginia, most English walnut trees died before reaching maturity. Walnut lovers turned to the black walnut, a species native to eastern North America. The nut had an extraordinarily tough shell and a somewhat oily taste. Even so, Native Americans had made use of the black walnut for about four thousand years. Some people extracted and boiled the sap of walnut trees to make a sweetener. The Mound Builders of Ohio and Indiana, whose culture flourished between 100 B.C. and A.D. 600, carved black walnut shells into animal shapes.

On the western side of the Rocky Mountains, the English walnut found a home in Oregon and California. Spanish priests founding **missions** in California established groves of the tall trees in the eighteenth century. The gray wool uniforms worn by the South's Confederate army during the Civil War (1861–1865) were known as "butternut gray." The dye came from a North American walnut, *J. cinerea*, known commonly as the butternut because of its oily-tasting kernels.

In 1867 a nurseryman named Joseph Sexton established a nursery in Santa Barbara, California, where he planted walnut seeds purchased in San Francisco. Evidently three of these seeds grew into trees that produced excellent walnuts with softer shells than most walnuts. The offspring of these trees formed the basis of southern California's new commercial walnut business. By the 1880s, walnut growers were prospering. In 1912 many of these growers came together to form a cooperative called the California Walnut Growers Association to produce and process walnuts. Beginning in the 1930s, southern California began to shift from a largely agricultural region to a booming urban center. Walnut growers moved northward as urbanization took off. By 1952 the cooperative had moved its base to Stockton, California, and had become Diamond Walnut Growers, Inc.

In modern times, Diamond Walnut Growers, Inc., is the world's largest walnut processor. Members of the cooperative grow about half of the walnuts in California, the only U.S. state to commercially raise walnuts. Diamond Walnut Growers, Inc., boasts a processing plant that covers seventy-five acres. During the six-week autumn harvest season, the installation receives over eight million walnuts every day. The nut cracking machines can handle more than one million pounds a day. Twenty-five trucks carry forty-two thousand-pound loads of walnuts from the plant every day. And on a daily basis, walnuts fill about forty huge containers. Each container can hold about forty thousand pounds. Massive container ships take about 43 percent of the co-op's walnuts overseas to Japan, Germany, Italy, and other international destinations.

A walnut nursery owner, Joseph Sexton, lounges in front of his California home in 1885.

It's a Fact!

"From soup to nuts" is an old-fashioned American expression that means about the same as "the whole enchilada." In other words, everything. A formal American meal once started with soup, and nuts followed dessert to end the meal.

Raising Walnuts

Walnut trees, like pecan trees, begin in nurseries. California walnut growers plant young grafted trees about thirty feet apart. Most of the trees begin producing nuts at about six years of age. Workers regularly prune and irrigate the young trees. Many orchards grow **cover crops,** such as barley, as natural fertilizer for the soil. Growers plant these cover crops in October and plow them into the soil in spring.

Since walnut trees carry both male and female flowers, they self-**pollinate** in the spring breezes. The short stubby female flowers are hard to spot, but the male flowers hang heavily on a stalk known as a catkin. The fruits that form from the female blossoms resemble clusters of small, green rugby balls. At the end of summer,

The walnut is monolithic. This means the tree has both male and female flowers.

A Greek couple gathers walnuts on the island of Crete.

the green hull shrivels and begins to pull back from the nutshell, signaling that harvest-time is near.

From September to November, workers sweep the ground under the trees moving the mechanical sweepers carefully to avoid damaging the trees' roots and trunks. Then workers run mechanical shakers into the orchards. An operator uses a windrowing machine to rake the nuts into rows for collection by a mechanical picker. The device grabs the nuts and shakes loose leaves and twigs. Other machines wash the nuts and remove the hulls that haven't shriveled away. At this point, the walnuts must be quickly dried to prevent the possibility of molding. Most walnuts are placed in mechanical dehydrators (drying machines).

Workers separate the dried nuts into categories depending on the quality of each nut. The best and biggest walnuts will be sold in the shell, or "in-shell," as it is called in the nut business. These nuts are placed in steel tanks and then treated with methyl bromide, a poisonous gas that kills insects such as mites and aphids. Next the nuts move on conveyors through a high-tech electronic sorting system and then into a bleach solution that leaves the walnut shells a uniform shade of tan. After being dried again, workers check samples to ensure the quality of the nuts. Finally machines package the walnuts into one-pound and two-pound bags.

A tree shaker loosens ripe walnuts from the tree.

About 70 percent of all California walnuts are sold shelled. These nuts are sorted into six different sizes. A device designed not to damage the kernel cracks each nutshell. A conveyer belt carries the kernels as they are electronically scanned for bits of shell. Once all stray bits of shell are removed, machines sort the walnuts by color and pack them into cans, bags, or cartons.

Walnut Wonders

Coffee cakes, tea breads, cookies, brownies, hot fudge sundaes, turkey dressing, and cakes all welcome walnuts in North America. The Lady Baltimore cake is a layered creation filled with raisins and walnuts, covered with boiled white frosting. The cake took off as a trendy dessert soon after being described in a popular American novel of that name in 1906.

Ethnic walnut dishes abound in the United States. *Rojik,* an Armenian specialty popular in New England, is homemade fruit leather made with grape juice, flour, and walnuts. The cook threads walnut halves onto a two-foot-long string, then dips the string again and again into the hot mix of juice, flour, and walnut. After the well-dipped strings cool down, the cook rolls them in powdered sugar. Rojik can be stored easily. Serbian Americans enjoy walnut rolls that star two pounds of ground walnuts. Slovenians specialize in *potica,* a type of strudel that features walnuts, raisins, and rum.

In the Asian country of Georgia, a favorite dish is *satsiui,* cold chicken in walnut sauce. Iranians delight in a dish called *fesenjan,* walnut sauce with pomegranate juice served atop chicken or duck.

Walnut and pumpkin pudding is a popular sweet dish from Iraq. Pumpkin chunks are glazed with sugar syrup, mixed with chopped walnuts, and served with cream or yogurt. Another Middle Eastern specialty, *qtayif* is a kind of light pancake often filled with ground walnuts and cinnamon. In the United States, cooks add chopped walnuts to chocolate chip cookies. And of course roasted, salted walnuts make an ever-popular, delicious snack. The Portuguese often prefer their local walnuts fresh from the shell and inserted in the middle of a perfectly ripe fig.

A street merchant in Istanbul, Turkey, offers walnuts among his goods.

More shelled walnuts are sold worldwide for baking than all other kinds of nuts combined.

What's in a Name?

Both the Greeks and the Romans saw an immediate resemblance between the walnut and the human head, including the brain. The outer covering or fruit around the walnut is like the scalp. The nutshell is the skull. And inside? Crack a walnut and remove the kernel. You'll see what looks like a tiny human brain, two hemispheres of twisted matter. Based on these observations, the Greeks named the walnut *caryon*, from the Greek word *kara*, meaning "head." The Romans dubbed the walnut "royal nut of the gods," because they perceived it to be far superior to everyday nuts such as acorns, chestnuts, and beechnuts. Why? Probably because walnuts cost much more.

Fifth-century Saxon invaders in England named the nut they found there "walnut." *Walnut* means "foreign or Celtic nut." Traditionally, Persian traders supplied the walnut, so most English-speakers referred to it as the Persian walnut. But British sailors spread

The Black Walnut

The black walnut, the most prized hardwood in the United States, is the tallest of the walnut family of trees, stretching as high as 150 feet. The black walnut grows wild in many parts of the United States. If you have one in your yard, your family may crack the rock-hard shells by running a car back and forth over the nuts spread on the drive. Black walnuts are harvested and processed commercially in Missouri and Alabama. Many bakers prize the black walnut over the English, especially at Thanksgiving and Christmas. Its flavor blends beautifully with flour, sugar, cinnamon, and butter. People carve the wood into clocks, bowls, and other items. The strong wood is also used for gunstocks and furniture.

Europeans once believed that witches danced around walnut trees at sundown.

the nut, so the Persian walnut became known as the English walnut.

Walnut Lore

In times past, Europeans tended to view the walnut as a bad tree with evil influence. A plentiful harvest of walnuts was considered to be a sign of a cold winter ahead. But walnuts could also have good influences. According to folklore, if someone picks a walnut leaf on a certain night and places it in your left boot, you will fall in love with that person!

Waste Not, Walnut!

Nothing is wasted with walnuts. Fibers, shells, and the bits of kernel still lodged in shells are ground into mash, then pressed to extract the oil for paints. Processors turn the remaining pancakelike substance into animal feed.

Meanwhile, other industries use those shells not invited to be part of the "mash" as filler in a range of products from tiles to glue. Some are ground into a fine powder and added to insecticides (poisons to kill insects). Walnut shells even fuel some processing plants.

Walnut trees supply wood that people craft into a variety of useful objects, including these shoes.

Dig In!

BROWNIES
(12 SERVINGS)

¼ cup butter
2 ounces of semi-sweet baking chocolate
½ cup sugar
½ cup flour
1 teaspoon vanilla
½ cup chopped walnuts
¼ cup chocolate chips

These tasty squares combine everyone's favorite chocolate and vanilla with the crunch of walnuts. Preheat the oven to 325°. Place the butter and the chocolate squares into a small glass dish. Microwave until the chocolate and butter are melted, or for about two minutes, and stir to blend. You can also use the stove to melt the butter and chocolate. Put the ingredients in a small saucepan over low heat, and carefully stir them as they melt.

Scrape the butter and chocolate mixture into a bowl. Add the sugar, flour, vanilla, and walnuts. Mix the ingredients until they are well blended. Add the chocolate chips. Pour the mixture into a greased eight-inch square pan. Bake the brownies for twenty to thirty minutes. (Check to see if the brownies are done by sticking a fork into the brownies. Take them out of the oven first! If the fork's tines are clean, the brownies are done.) After you carefully take the brownies out of the oven, cut them into squares while they're still hot. Wait until they've cooled down before you begin munching!

Almonds
[*Prunus amygdalus*]

What has blooms like a peach tree and forms a fruit that looks like a peach but is not eaten? The almond tree. This lovely tree is closely related to the peach, the plum, and the apricot. In springtime the small tree's graceful branches are coated with delicate pink flowers. Later in spring, rich green leaves appear. Tiny toothlike indentations edge the lancelike leaves. The almond tree's fruit is a soft green, enclosing the almond kernel's distinctive pockmarked shell.

Ancient Almonds

Botanists believe the almond to be a prehistoric hybrid, the offspring of two unrelated plants that has characteristics of both parents. In the case of the almond, parentage is unknown. Experts trace the almond's origins to the Anatolian Peninsula (the site of modern-day Turkey). Archaeologists have found almond remains in ancient sites in Cyprus and Greece. The almond was a familiar food in the Middle East by about 1700 B.C.—it was even mentioned in the Old Testament of the Bible.

Almonds resemble the pit of the peach, to which the nuts are related.

When there are plentiful dates and almonds, there is prosperity and long life.

—A Lebanese saying

About 300 B.C., Theophrastus, an ancient Greek scientist and follower of the philosopher Aristotle, wrote of the almond in his *History of Plants*. Little is known as to how ancient peoples ate the almond, but historians guess that the Greeks ate it fresh. Some probably ground the nut into flour. By 200 B.C., the almond made its way to Italy—the Romans called it "the Greek nut." Roman farmers planted almond trees throughout the Mediterranean region and in most of the Roman Empire. Roman walnut eaters may have created a recipe for delicious sugared almonds.

Almonds All Over

Newly united by the religion of Islam in the late A.D. 600s, people from the Arabian Peninsula forged the Islamic Empire, which included parts of what would become Iraq and Iran. There the Arab newcomers encountered the almond tree and learned to appreciate it. They planted the tree across their empire, which by the 700s encompassed the Middle East, North Africa, and the Iberian Peninsula (modern-day Spain and Portugal).

By 716 records in a Norman monastery (a religious home for monks) in northern France were mentioning the almond tree. Beginning about 1200, records from Verdun, France, noted the giving of sugared almonds to bishops. Records also show that this treat was a common product in several cities of northern France, including Paris and Nancy. The cities are still known for their sugared almonds.

In the late Middle Ages, the Islamic Empire controlled Jerusalem, a holy city for Judaism, Islam, and Christianity. The Roman Catholic pope Urban II commanded loyal Christians to capture this holy city. The mostly European warriors, known as Crusaders, marched to Jerusalem and won it after a bloody battle in 1099. The Crusaders encountered more than just battle fatigue. They were exposed to tasty Arab cookery, which included sauces laced with chopped or

As in ancient times, almond trees dot the landscape of northern France.

Garden Almonds

Jordan almonds—large almonds often coated with pastel-colored candy—have nothing to do with the country itself. French-speakers called this delicacy "*amandes des jardins*," or garden almonds. Somewhere along the line, the word "*jardin*" became transformed into Jordan.

In the late 1700s, residents of missions in California ate almonds.

powdered almonds. Soldiers sampled sweet treats such as nougat, a sugar candy filled with almonds. The Crusaders also enjoyed marzipan, a sweet almond paste flavored with rose water or orange rind. (Rose water is an intensely sweet liquid extracted from rose petals.) Cooks modeled the confection into fanciful shapes, such as fruits and pigs.

Marzipan delights and their recipes returned home with the Crusaders. In England in 1387, King Richard II invited two thousand guests to an elaborate dinner. For dessert? A four-foot-square and three-foot-high marzipan castle, complete with moat and drawbridges. Though the English had been growing almond trees since Roman times, they ate imported almonds. England's climate is not warm enough to encourage the tree to bear fruit.

Crusaders may also have learned from the Arabs the technique of creating "milk" from blanched, soaked, and pounded almonds. This substitute for cow's milk was common in Europe for generations and was a key ingredient in many French sauces until the 1700s.

In the late 1500s and 1600s, Spaniards carried the almond to their colonies (settlements) in the Americas. Spanish priests establishing missions in California in the late 1700s included almonds in their plantings.

Settlers along the East Coast tried to grow almonds in the early nineteenth century. Because the almond blooms in February, the flower is easily killed by frost—common that time of year in the region. Almond growing on a commercial scale just wasn't reliable.

But trees from a New York nursery were successful pioneers in California soil. By the 1850s, almond trees took root in the San Joaquin Valley. In modern times, California almonds represent a $1 billion industry.

This California almond grove is in full bloom in early spring. By fall the almonds will be fully formed *(inset)*.

These almond trees are ready for harvest. Here, a mechanical tree shaker tends to an almond tree.

Almond Growing

California produces 735 million pounds of almonds each year. The state supplies 100 percent of commercially grown U.S. almonds. And that crop provides more than 70 percent of the world's almonds. California almonds are the United States's seventh largest food export. Germany is California's biggest foreign customer, purchasing 25 percent of the exported almonds. Japan buys 12 percent of the exports. And Spain is the third major customer for the U.S. product. Spain is the world's second-largest producer of almonds, with over 160 million pounds each year. Spain's production is primarily from groves along the country's Mediterranean seacoast.

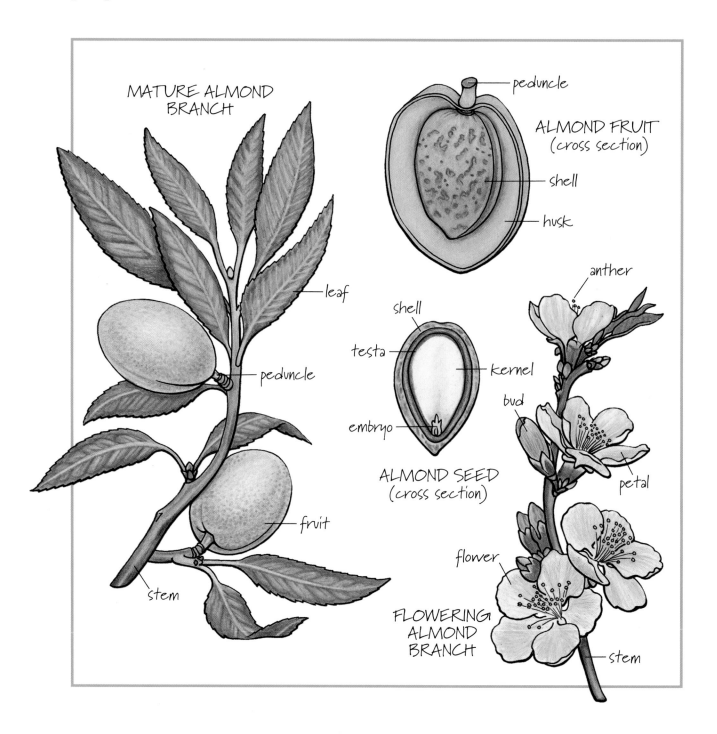

MATURE ALMOND
BRANCH

leaf

peduncle

fruit

stem

ALMOND FRUIT
(cross section)

peduncle

shell

husk

ALMOND SEED
(cross section)

shell

testa

kernel

embryo

anther

bud

petal

flower

FLOWERING
ALMOND
BRANCH

stem

As with many other nut trees, almonds grow from grafted seedlings. Many almond varieties are grafted onto peach rootstock. The young trees are planted about twenty-five to thirty feet apart in irrigated orchards. Over 50 percent of California almond trees are of the variety *nonpareil,* a French word meaning "without equal." The nonpareil has a soft, easily opened shell. But each orchard has at least two varieties of almond trees. Almond trees aren't self-pollinating, and they must be pollinated across varieties.

As soon as the swollen pink almond buds open, farmers bring beehives to the sweetly scented almond orchard. The bees fly from blossom to blossom. As they travel, they pick up and deposit pollen. The busy bees must introduce the pollen of one almond variety to the blossoms of the other.

The fuzzy fruits begin to form in late spring (as the tree's leaves appear) and usually begin to split open in July. By early autumn, the fruit is fully split and ready to harvest. Machines sweep the ground clean under the almond trees. Mechanical tree shakers knock the ripe nuts to the ground, where nuts dry for five to ten days. If it rains, workers move the nuts to a mechanical dryer. A worker uses a sweeper to brush the nuts into tidy rows. Another person maneuvers a pickup machine, or harvester, which easily gathers the nuts and discards leaves and twigs. Next the harvester empties the nuts into carts, which empty into truck trailers.

 # To Your Health!

Almonds, like most nuts, are superior protectors of the heart. Researchers think this may be because nuts contain magnesium, Vitamin E, and monounsaturated fat. Almonds also boast calcium, which builds strong bones and teeth. The fiber in almonds and other foods is a carbohydrate the body needs for good digestion. Fiber expands in the stomach, helping eaters feel full, and passes quickly through the body. Protein, of which almonds have plenty, forms healthy skin, hair, and nails. Protein helps maintain the body and repair tissue.

Almonds are used in many Indian dishes, such as *shahi korma*, lamb with almonds and yogurt.

When delivered to the processing plant, a few almonds in every batch are cracked open and inspected. Then the batch is graded according to size and quality. Electronic sorters remove any foreign objects or defective nuts. Then hullers remove any remaining fruit from the stone. A tiny percentage of almonds will be sold in the shell. But most almonds are marketed whole, sliced, chopped, or slivered. Machines crack and remove the shells, then clean and package the nuts. Some nuts are shipped to candy manufacturers. Others go to companies that roast, salt, and further process the almonds. All sizes of bags and cans head to markets around the world.

Eating the Almond

In Lebanon you can buy and eat fresh almonds that haven't yet formed their nuts. Inside the future almond is a jelly, evidently prized by those who like to get in on things from the beginning. Israeli cooks choose slivered almonds to top their *ugat dvash,* a honey cake flavored with spices and citrus. Travelers to Syria can taste ball-shaped almond candies built around maraschino cherries. They can also sample a sweet treat called *samsa,* made with ground almonds, pastry, and honey. In neighboring Jordan, cooks use almonds for a similar dish. Popular in Iraq, *roz bil tamar* is dates, raisins, and almonds atop rice.

Candied almonds are one of the many ways to enjoy the nut.

A nut seller in Calcutta, India, show his wares at a bus stop.

A dish common in northern India is *shahi korma*, lamb with almonds and yogurt. The seasoned lamb is marinated in yogurt and then slowly cooked with cream, slivered almonds, and lots of garlic. Traditional wedding cakes in Great Britain may be frosted with icing containing almond paste, to symbolize the combination of the bitter and the sweet common to the married state.

Almond milk is a specialty of Morocco. Served chilled, the drink combines finely ground roasted almonds with sugar, milk, and grated orange rind. And in Greece, *skordalia* (sauce made from ground almonds, potatoes, garlic, lemon juice, and olive oil) is served on vegetables or meat. In Málaga, Spain, cooks add extra garlic, white grapes, and ground almonds to the cold vegetable soup *gazpacho*. Spaniards also eat almond cake topped with powdered sugar. In South America, a Chilean dish called *coliflor in salsa de almendra* spruces up cauliflower with a succulent sauce that includes ground and chopped almonds flavored with nutmeg.

Throughout northern Europe, the almond flavors cookies and pastries. *Lebkuchen*, the thick spice cookie from Germany, always includes almonds. Another treat is *obsttorte*, a

Marzipan pastries

It's a Fact!

In Denmark the person who finds the single almond buried in the traditional Christmas Eve rice pudding wins a prize, which is usually a pink marzipan pig.

fruit tart with sides covered in roasted, slivered almonds. Probably the best-known almond pastry item in Germany is marzipan. As in the days of the Crusaders, modern-day confectioners mold marzipan into animals, fruits, people, and trees. Lübeck, Germany, is a key manufacturer of marzipan. In the Algarve area of Portugal, marzipan is shaped into fanciful fish. In Norway and Denmark, professional chefs create towering *kransekage*. These special celebratory cakes are made almost entirely from marzipan. Ordered for weddings and birthdays, the cakes often tower more than two feet high. Pastry chefs roll marzipan flat and use it as a covering for cakes or mix it with jam to use as a cookie filling.

A traveler to Sweden once observed that the Swedes use almonds the way North Americans use chocolate—in cookies, pastries, and cakes. In addition, Swedes from the province of Småland love a pudding-

During Christmastime in Germany, children eat tiny, realistic-looking vegetables and fruits made from marzipan.

The Bitter Almond

If you can take the bitter with the sweet, then you should be happy with the almond family. Bitter almonds, a different variety from the sweet almonds people eat, have a role to play, too. Most cultivated bitter almonds are processed for their oil, which is used in skin creams and to flavor liqueurs. In the process of extracting the oil, the poisonous hydrocyanic (prussic) acid is removed as well. The presence of hydrocyanic acid doesn't keep people from enjoying the taste of bitter almonds in very small amounts. Bakers in some countries mix bitter almonds with the sweet, but the United States bans the sale of bitter almonds.

like cheesecake called *ostkaka*. It's made with more than a cup of ground almonds, along with ample measures of cream, milk, eggs, flour, and sugar. An unusual dish popular in Sweden is *nyponsoppa*. This cold fruit soup is made of rose hips, served with whipped cream and sprinkled with almonds.

North Americans eat marzipan as well but are more likely to snack on roasted almonds, chomp down on them in candy bars, or sauté them in butter to serve on trout. Some folks eat almond butter spread on sandwiches or crackers.

Almonds make a tasty snack.

Magical Branches

Almonds have long been connected with hope, good luck, and magic, perhaps because blossoms appear suddenly on the tree's bare branches. In the Middle Ages, Europeans looking for underground sources of water used fresh fork-shaped branches from the almond tree as "divining rods." (Divining means figuring out or discovering.) The seeker held the branch horizontally over the ground. When the diviner walked around, the stick would quiver. Diviners believed that the force of the hidden water pulled the forked stick down over the source of water. This practice continues in many parts of the world, including the United States.

Hi-Tech Almonds

Some dairy farmers feed their milkers pulverized almond hulls. The shells are ground up as filler for cattle feed, as bedding for dairy cows, or as part of charcoal briquettes. In the 1980s, almond shells from the California Almond Growers' plant in Sacramento provided electricity for the processing plant and for thousands of homes in the area.

A child in Mumbai (formerly known as Bombay), India, buys almonds from a streetside vendor.

Dig In!

ROZ BIL TAMAR
(4 SERVINGS)

2 tablespoons butter
1 cup whole almonds
1 cup dates with pits removed
1 cup raisins
1 cup cooked rice
1 teaspoon rose water

An Iraqi dish, rice with dates and almonds is a flavorful favorite.

Over low heat, melt the butter in a large saucepan. When the melted butter bubbles gently, add the almonds. While stirring constantly, fry the almonds for one or two minutes. Keep stirring as you add the dates and the raisins. (You may need to add an extra half-teaspoon of butter to make sure the ingredients are coated.)

After a *few minutes,* the fruit will swell up. Put the cooked rice on top of the fruit and nuts and stir well. Reduce the heat to very low. Stirring often, cook the mixture for ten minutes or until the rice is hot.

Just before serving the roz bil tamar, sprinkle on the rose water. Top the dish with a few extra almonds.

Hint: An Asian grocery store is a good place to look for rose water. If you can't find it, use a teaspoon of grated orange rind instead.

Pistachios

[*Pistacia vera*]

The pistachio is a Middle Eastern nut that makes naturally green desserts possible. The pistachio nut grows on a rugged tree that is cousin to the mango, cashew, sumac, and poison oak. Thriving in heat, the pistachio tree grows only to a height of about twenty-five feet and flourishes in rocky dry soil. Its hollylike leaves grow in threes. Its nuts grow in clusters resembling grapes. Pistachios probably trace their origins to Iran and nearby areas.

In the past, pistachio shells were dyed red to cover any blemishes.

If it were not for its color, the pistachio nut might have remained virtually unknown outside its home territory.

—Waverley Root

Pistachios were found in the ruins of Beidha, an ancient settlement in modern-day Jordan *(left)*. Pistachio trees grew in the fabled Hanging Gardens of Babylon *(below)*, around 700 B.C. King Nebuchadnezzar built the series of terraced gardens high above a river to cheer up his wife, Amytis. She had found Babylon's flat landscape dreary.

Ancient Pistachios

People have eaten the pistachio for more than eight thousand years. Thousands of years ago, a fire swept through a clay and mud brick settlement called Beidha in what would become Jordan. In 1965 archaeologists at Beidha discovered a forty-pound batch of pistachios in a large basket that was carbon dated to 6760 B.C.

Pistachios are mentioned in the Bible's Old Testament. Scholars believe pistachios were the nuts Jacob's son carried into Egypt, according to Genesis (the first book of the Bible). Legend relates that the Queen of Sheba took all the pistachios produced in her kingdom of Assyria for herself and her court in 950 B.C.

Pistachios had traveled from Syria to Rome by about A.D. 50. There is little documented history of pistachios after this time, until the pistachio pops up in sixteenth-century records that show the nut had reached England, possibly from France.

Pistachios in America

Pistachios reached the United States in 1854, when a commissioner of patents, Charles Mason, sent seeds to California and Texas. The result is lost to history. But in the 1880s, imported pistachios caught on in New York City. In the 1920s and 1930s, vending machines sold pistachios—charging a nickel for a dozen. The nutshells tended to become discolored and bruised in the all-by-hand harvesting process, so sellers began to dye the shells red or white.

The first hero of the California commercial pistachio business was William E. Whitehorse. A botanist and plant sleuth, Whitehorse spent six months in Iran and central Asia in 1929 gathering pistachio seeds and advice about pistachio growing. He returned with a burlap bag filled with twenty pounds of seeds from ninety different sources. Working in Chico, California, during the early 1930s, he developed cultivars. He dubbed a large, easy-to-open cultivar "Kerman" after an Iranian city. By 1950 Kerman had become the star pistachio and ultimately became the variety most grown in California.

Demand for pistachios in the United States took off during this period. California growers found they couldn't compete with Middle Eastern farmers, where workers earned less than workers did in the United States. So early on, California growers decided to use machines to help harvest and process pistachios. With machines, farmers had fewer workers to pay, so it cost them less to grow pistachios.

Nuts, including pistachios, are sold in bulk at cooperative supermarkets.

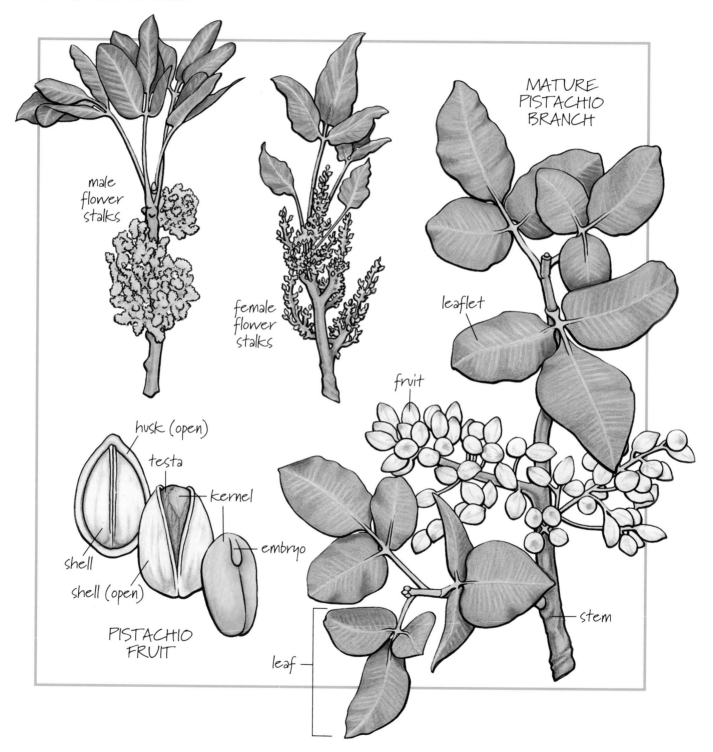

male flower stalks

female flower stalks

MATURE PISTACHIO BRANCH

leaflet

husk (open)

testa

kernel

shell

embryo

shell (open)

PISTACHIO FRUIT

fruit

stem

leaf

This bakery in Lebanon has a variety of sweets made with pistachios.

Growing Pistachios

Arid countries such as Turkey, Syria, Afghanistan, and Iran suit the pistachio best. It also grows in the Mediterranean countries of Italy, Tunisia, and Greece, as well as in Pakistan and India. And since the 1970s, the pistachio has found new homes in California, New Mexico, and Arizona. California pistachio growers may produce almost 200 million pounds of the green nuts one year but only 100 million the next year. The harvest varies so much because the trees are biennial (they bear a full crop only every other year). But under excellent conditions, the trees can produce for centuries.

Pistachio trees raised in nurseries grow from grafts of selected species. Pistachios are dioecious (the trees come in male and female varieties). Most growers plant one male tree per eight to ten female trees. Wind

It's a Fact!

The pistachio's uniqueness is its green color. Ancient Persians used several nuts, including pistachios, mixed into desserts. Arabs copied them and brought the treat to medieval Spain. This borrowing may be how green crept into after-dinner pleasures such as pistachio ice cream and pistachio nougat candy.

Blanks

A curious feature of the pistachio is that the shell forms first—the kernel gradually grows inside. Sometimes a kernel doesn't form. The result is a nutless nutshell known as a "blank." Blanks don't fetch much in the marketplace.

Two workers clean and separate freshly harvested pistachios.

carries pollen from the male to the tiny flowers of the females. Each row of trees is set about thirty feet apart in deep, well-drained soils. Within the rows, ten to fifteen feet separate the trees. Those who raise pistachios are patient. The trees begin to produce after seven years or so, but they don't reach full production until they're teenagers.

Pick a Peck of Pistachios

At harvesttime workers operating specialized machines shake the fully ripe nuts from the tree. These harvesters embrace each tree with metal arms and shake the mature nuts onto canvas conveyor belts. They throw out unwanted twigs and leaves and then toss the pistachios into bins. One tree can be harvested in less than a minute. With eighty-two thousand acres of pistachios to be harvested in California, time is money.

The first twenty-five hours off the tree are crucial for California pistachios. To keep the nuts from becoming stained and blemished, the nuts must be hulled (shelled) quickly. In September and October, California growers run their harvesting and processing operations twenty-four hours a day. The nuts are pulled between rough, rubberized belts that shuck the thin hulls. The nuts drop into tanks of water where the mature nuts sink and move to the next process. Empty shells, known as blanks, float and are tossed out. The nuts are washed and dried. Blemished nuts are sorted electronically and may be dyed. The rest of the nuts are graded into four different sizes. Most are roasted and salted right in the shell. The shells usually split naturally, just before harvest, as they hang on the tree. Most of the nut, therefore, is protected with its own natural packaging. The eater makes the final move of splitting apart the shell with a finger and tossing the nut down the hatch.

Purists insist the smaller nuts grown in the Middle East and harvested by hand have more flavor. California produces a larger, more attractive pistachio.

Hand Labor Is Hard Labor

Pistachios became a valuable export in the early 1900s, so countries like Turkey and Iran began farming the nut on a grand scale. Pistachios grow throughout the driest parts of Iran. Iranians consider Kerman the pistachio capital of the country. The town, in southeastern Iran, is also famous for its beautiful carpets.

Traditional harvesting of pistachios involves the labor of many women. In remote regions of Turkey and Iran, female workers may pick the ripe nuts off the tree by hand. Usually workers use poles to knock the nuts to the burlap-covered ground. Most pistachios dry in the sun with the hulls still attached, then soak in water. Then the women pinch the nuts to slip off the hulls.

Pistachios often arrive with their shells partially open.

To Your Health!

Packed with protein, pistachios contain potassium and fiber. And they're high in polyunsaturated fats, the so-called "good fats" that may reduce harmful cholesterol levels.

Dig In!

PISTACHIO PASTA SALAD
(8 SERVINGS)

The salad:
6 ounces rotini pasta, or some other small pasta of your choice
1 cup pea pods
2 cups fresh spinach, torn
¼ cup chopped pistachios
1 cup chopped tomato
A grinding of pepper
A sprinkle of fresh Parmesan cheese

The oregano dressing:
¼ cup olive oil
¼ cup red wine vinegar
¾ teaspoon crushed oregano
1 garlic clove, crushed and minced

A new American use for the exotic pistachio in a delicious pasta salad. Cook the pasta in boiling, salted water until done. (See package directions.) While the pasta is cooking, make the dressing by combining all of the dressing's ingredients in a large bowl. When the pasta is cooked, turn off the heat.

Remove it from the boiling water with a slotted spoon. Put the pasta into the bowl with the dressing and stir until the pasta is well coated with dressing. Leave it on the counter until the pasta cools to room temperature. It won't take long.

Turn on the heat under the water. When the water is boiling again, toss in the pea pods for about thirty seconds. Drain the pea pods and let them cool. Then add the pea pods, spinach, pistachios, and chopped tomatoes to the pasta. Stir them together and add a bit of pepper. Then sprinkle the blend with Parmesan cheese, and you're ready to serve a delicious salad!

People in Middle Eastern countries munch on pistachios sold by street vendors.

The pistachios dry in the sun before being packed into burlap bags to take to markets just down the road or across the world.

Pistachio Eating

Imagine walking the narrow streets of an Iranian bazaar as businesses close for the day. You may find your feet crunching on discarded pistachio shells underfoot. Pistachios are the number one snack food in Iran and in many other Middle Eastern countries. Snackers may leave trails of shells behind them.

A typical Iranian sweet is *halva*, made with sugar, oil, flour, saffron, and rose water. The treat is topped with a mix of pistachios and slivered almonds.

In northern India, diners with a sweet tooth enjoy *kalfi*, a frozen milk-based dessert involving pistachios, almonds, and rose water. Another speciality of the region is *gajar halva*, or carrots cooked with raisins and chopped pistachios. A unique sweet yogurt dish known as *shrikhand* combines saffron, sugar, and milk. Cooks top shrikhand with pistachios.

Acorns

The acorn is one of the first nuts with which many young people become familiar. These nuts, which fall from the oak tree, are native to the northern temperate zones of Asia, North America, and Europe. Acorns are usually round or elongated, green or brown.

The acorn was a special favorite of the Ahwahneechee of California's Yosemite Valley. The Ahwahneechee developed ways of storing, drying, and then processing acorns into meal or fine flour. Oaks come in many different varieties, but the Ahwahneechee preferred the highly nutritious nuts of the black oak, *Quercus kelloggii*.

They gathered the second of the two "falls" of nuts in the autumn—the first batch usually contained sick or damaged nuts. In late September, the second and largest grouping of nuts would fall. The women would carefully dry the nuts outdoors for a few weeks. Then they moved the acorns to special granaries (storage areas). After about a year of storage, women cracked the nuts with a stone and rubbed off the acorns' skins. Women pounded the nuts into meal, which they sifted.

Acorns and acorn flour contain a bitter compound called tannin. Cooks leached (washed with water) the flour to clear away the bitter taste. After it dried, the leached flour was ready to be cooked into mush or flat, round cakes. Native American cooks placed red-hot stones from a fire into tightly woven baskets filled with *nuppa*, a mush of acorn flour and water. In modern times, people cook nuppa in stainless steel pots on stoves. And they prepare acorns a more modern way. They crack the shells with a hammer and grind the kernels in a blender or food processor.

This picture from the early 1900s shows children selling acorns.

Baklava was a delicacy in ancient Greece and is still a popular dessert in modern times.

U.S. nibblers each eat more than two pounds of nuts, including pistachios, a year!

Pistachio ice cream, green from the nut itself, is a seasonal favorite in U.S pistachio-growing areas. It pops up at ice cream stores across the country, but in a version usually greened with a dash of food coloring.

Throughout the Middle East and Greece, pastry makers create *baklava*, a favorite sweet, sticky dessert. Assembled in layers like lasagna, baklava features about twenty layers of paper-thin pastry separated by ground pistachios or walnuts. Brushed with butter and baked, the cooked pastry is covered in a honey and lemon syrup before serving.

Cashews
[*Anacardium occidentale*]

The cashew is an unusual nut. It dangles from a pear-shaped cashew apple (no relation to a regular apple) like a frivolous afterthought. But there is nothing light and frilly about the cashew. Its nutshell contains cashew nutshell liquid (CNSL), which is toxic. CNSL can irritate skin more than poison ivy does. In fact, the cashew is a cousin to poison ivy, poison sumac, and poison oak. But cashews are also relatives of the mango and the pistachio.

A hearty evergreen tree, the cashew thrives in the heat of the **tropics.** It grows wild or can be easily cultivated. Reaching fifty feet tall, the tree has crooked branches and a rough-barked twisting trunk. The cashew puts forth perfumed yellow-pink flowers.

Cashew nuts are delicious shelled and unsalted.

A man cannot marry if he does not have cashews.

—A Jamaican proverb

Historically Speaking

The cashew probably first evolved near the equator in northeastern Brazil. The native people there harvested the tree for the cashew apple and the nut. A French naturalist named Thevet made a drawing of the tree in 1558. He showed the harvest and collection of the juice of the cashew apple. Thevet described the taste of the cooked nut as "excellent."

The Portuguese, who colonized Brazil, and the Spaniards, who colonized the rest of South America, carried the cashew to other parts of the world. Spaniards moved cashews by ship from Mexico to the Philippines in the 1570s. The Portuguese sailed with the nut to East Africa and to their colony of Goa, India, in about 1590. From Goa, either birds or people soon carried the cashew into southern India and Indonesia.

Brazilian weavers made this colorful tapestry. The native Brazilians often ate cashews with their meals.

The outer covering of the cashew fruit contains an extremely caustic oil that must be burned off before the nut can be touched.

Cultivating Cashews

In modern times, the cashew grows in several African countries, including Kenya and Nigeria. Malaysia and Thailand produce cashews, too. India, more than 7,500 miles as the crow flies from Brazil, the cashew's homeland, is the world's cashew power. Mozambique and Tanzania take second and third place. (The United States grows no commercial crops of cashews.) In recent years, 95 percent of the world's cashew harvest came from trees growing wild. But what was once mainly a crop that grew wild is increasingly cultivated.

This is partly because cloning and grafting have helped growers introduce different varieties. And when planted about thirty-five feet apart in orchards, cashew trees prosper. They do require full sun, with between 50 and 110 inches of rain per year. But in order to thrive, the thirsty plants also need three or four dry months. The tropics—which have both rainy and dry seasons—provide these conditions.

A woman carefully waters a cashew nut tree in Ghana, a West African country that grows only a small amount of trees.

Workers in Brazil use string to bind harvested cashew apples *(left)*. These cashew apples are ready for harvest *(right)*.

In the third year of growth, the young cashew trees begin bearing nuts. By the seventh year, nut production is in full swing. When the tree blooms, fragrant pinkish yellow flowers appear in profusion. The cashew trees bloom for up to three months. As the tree's true fruit, the cashew nut develops from the flower. Next comes a swelling in the flower's stalk, which signals the growing cashew apple. Two months after flowering, the apple and nut are ready for harvest.

The cashew apple is edible.

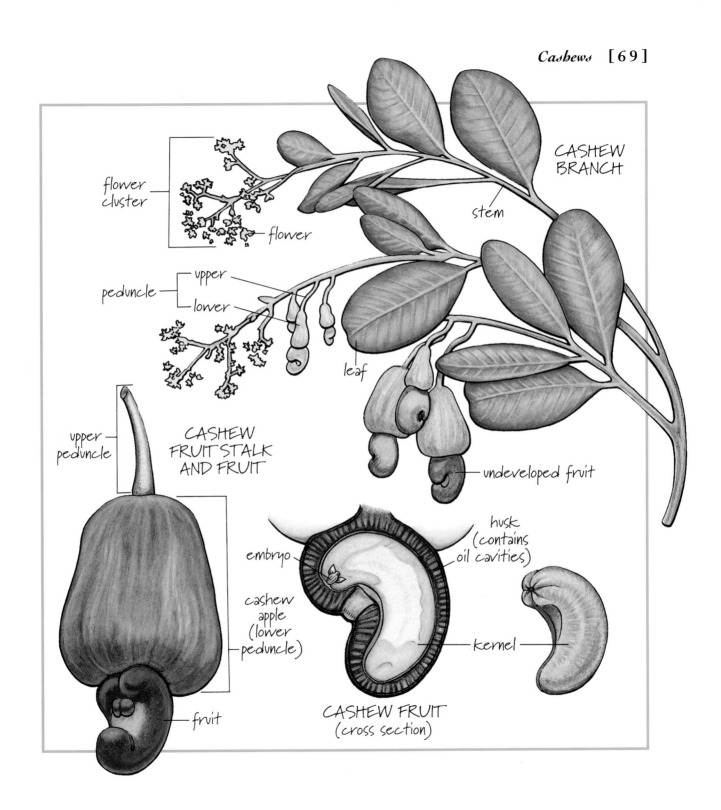

CASHEW BRANCH

flower cluster

flower

stem

peduncle
upper
lower

leaf

upper peduncle

CASHEW FRUIT STALK AND FRUIT

undeveloped fruit

husk (contains oil cavities)

embryo

cashew apple (lower peduncle)

kernel

fruit

CASHEW FRUIT (cross section)

Some growers cut the cashew apples from the tree so the apples won't fall to the ground and bruise. Growers who harvest only the nuts leave them on the tree to mature and fall on their own.

In Mozambique and India, workers do much of the cashew harvesting and processing by hand. Laborers rake the fallen nuts, which dry in the sun on bamboo mats or inside on well-swept floors. The nuts dry until they rattle when shaken. Then it's time to remove CNSL from the shell.

Some small processors roast the nuts in a sieve over a wood fire. The liquid falls through the sieve as the shells roast. This method can be dangerous for workers, who may breathe the irritating smoke into their lungs, causing damage. Larger processors use a method called solvent extraction. The nuts plunge into

To Your Health!

The cashew apple, although not widely eaten outside of Brazil and Asia, is remarkably high in Vitamin C. The Tikuna people of Amazonas, Brazil's northwestern state, use the juice to cure the flu. Brazilians add the fruit to shampoo as a scalp conditioner.

Cashew nuts are lower in fat than most other nuts. Cashews are only 72 percent fat, while almonds are 81 percent, and Brazil nuts are a whopping 92 percent fat. Cashews also supply fiber, protein, and B Vitamins.

Unpeeled cashews are individually weighed.

a chemical bath, which releases and captures CNSL. This process captures more than 80 percent of the liquid.

Once CNSL processing is complete, the nuts are ready to be shelled. In India small producers do this by hand—women open the nuts with wooden mallets and remove the kernels. The kernels dry in the sun, and then the workers rub the kernels between their fingers to take off the "skin," a thin outer covering.

Mechanized processors, many of which are in Africa, may run the nuts through cracking machines or through systems that use rotary (turning) blades. The devices break open and peel the cashews. The peeled cashews are then sorted, washed, and packed by hand into tin boxes and shipped in fifty-pound units to markets all over the world.

Cooking with Cashews

In the southern province of Ranong, Thailand, the cashew is a major crop. Each March the area holds a harvest celebration called the Sweet Cashew Fair. Thais eat the entire cashew, using the fruit in salads or with hot chilies. Even the edible leaves are frequently eaten raw in a spicy dipping sauce. *Yam Med Mamuang* is an appetizer made from fried and cooled cashews mixed with spicy chilies, green onions, shallots, and a squeeze of lime juice.

Cooks in the south of India add roasted

Cashews are a major crop in southern Thailand, where this factory is located.

Rice pilaf with cashews

A woman sells bags of cashews on the roadside.

Tupi Words

"Cashew" isn't the only word that comes from Tupi, the language of the Tupi Indians of Brazil. Many Tupi words changed a little as they were absorbed into other languages. The Tupi named a musical instrument a maraca. They called a tropical bird with a colorful beak a *tukána*, or a toucan. The Tupi named a mountain lion *sivasvarána*, which means "like a deer." The Tupi word became the English "cougar". Manioc (a Tupi word for cassava) can be shredded into grains called *tipioća* (tapioca), which is made into a tasty pudding. The Tupi called a bright flower a *pertima*, or petunia, and a tasty spice *kyinha*, or cayenne.

cashews to rice cooked in milk and brown sugar, making a sweet creamy dish called *payasam*. *Murgh biriani,* from the central part of the country, is a spicy coriander chicken dish topped with fried onions and cashews. Roasted cashews are used in a wide range of Indian rice dishes known as pilaf.

Dig In!

CASHEW NUTS PIRI-PIRI
(4 SERVINGS)

2 tablespoons olive oil
1 clove garlic, crushed
½ teaspoon chili powder
1 teaspoon fresh lemon juice
½ teaspoon salt
½ pound cashew nuts

This spicy sauce is the national dish of Mozambique, an East African nation. Heat the oil in a heavy pan and gently cook garlic and chili powder for two minutes. Then add lemon juice, salt, and cashews. Fry slowly, stirring constantly, until most of the sauce has coated the nuts. Serve the nuts as a snack. They're also delicious on top of baked potatoes or rice.

What's in a Name?

The name cashew comes originally from a Tupi word, *acaju*. Portuguese explorers in Brazil learned this term from the native Brazilian Tupi people. The Portuguese adopted the word and shortened it to *caju*, which became cashew in English.

High Tech

The use of CNSL in industry is on the rise. The automotive industry uses CNSL in brake linings and in clutch facings. Other industries add CNSL to paints, varnishes, and insulating materials. CNSL is also used in the cement, rubber, and paper industries.

Macadamias

[*Macadamia integrifolia*]

The macadamia tree is one of Australia's gifts to the world. The white, crunchy nut is one of the world's most desirable, in-demand treats. Growing to a height of forty-five to sixty feet, the trees have glossy green leaves that Hawaiians and Australians weave into holiday wreathes. Macadamia trees produce heavy stalks of sweetly scented pink or white flowers. These become fruit about one inch to one and a half inches in diameter. A brownish green husk encases the hard shell, which protects the delicious macadamia kernel. Two separate species of macadamia provide edible nuts. Macadamia trees can produce for as many as sixty years.

A native of Australia, the macadamia nut grows in places with tropical climates, such as Hawaii.

The cockatoo flew out and collected some nuts and scattered them around the mountain so the Baphal would have food. . . . When our people saw the nuts they called them Baphal's nuts.

—From the Aboriginal
Legend of the Baphal

[74]

Macadamia Mania

For generations, each autumn (March, in Australia) and winter the native or aboriginal people of Australia gathered the nuts of what many called the "Kindal Kindal." The trees grew on the eastern slopes of the Great Dividing Range, a mountain range that crosses subtropical areas of Queensland, a state in northeastern Australia. On Fraser Island off Australia's east coast, people knew the nuts as "Baphals." Macadamias thrived in northern New South Wales in eastern Australia. For the Aborigines, the nuts were a seasonal treat, not the mainstay of their diet.

In the 1700s, early British settlers of Australia may have sampled the nuts. But no one seems to have put a botanical label on the tree until 1857. That year an Australian botanist named Baron Ferdinand Von Mueller first came upon a tree that he couldn't identify. Von Mueller was the director of the Melbourne Botanic Gardens. Walter Hill, director of the Botanic Gardens at Brisbane, accompanied him. As Von Mueller had already collected over forty-five thousand plant specimens, he probably knew a new (to non-Aborigines) tree when he saw one. Von Mueller first described the tree botanically. He named it the macadamia for his good friend John Macadam, a young Scottish chemist who had died at sea traveling from Australia to New Zealand.

To Your Health!

Nuts used to be thought of as fat, fatter, and fattest—and all that fat was thought to be unhealthy. Although macadamias are indeed fatty, they're still good for you. Science is discovering that the macadamia's percentage of monounsaturated fat, 70 percent, is good for lowering blood cholesterol levels in the body.

Participants in an Australian study added six to twenty macadamia nuts to their diet each day. Results showed blood cholesterol levels lowered by 7 percent in just four weeks.

Aborigines in Queensland told Walter Hill that macadamias were poisonous, but he was curious about the nuts. Hill brought some nuts to his assistant at the Botanic Gardens and asked him to crack the stone-hard shells. A bit later, Hill was stunned to discover his assistant happily eating them. Hill tried some too, declared them delicious, and became a promoter of the tasty nut. In 1858 Hill planted what he believed to be the first cultivated macadamia on the shores of the Brisbane River. The Aborigines have a long history of plant selection and cultivation, however, so Hill's efforts may not really be the first.

Through the 1860s and 1870s, Hill encouraged growers to plant macadamias in New South Wales. During the same period, the Aborigines sold wild macadamia nuts to European settlers in Australia. An aboriginal elder known as King Jacky traded the tasty nuts for tobacco and rum.

The biggest event in macadamia history went virtually unnoticed. Sometime in 1882 or thereabouts, William H. Purvis brought seeds from Queensland to the U.S. territory of Hawaii. Purvis established young seedlings and planted them at Kukuihaele, a community on the big island of Hawaii.

In 1918 Walter Pierre Naquin, the manager of the Honokaa Sugar Company in Hawaii, saw macadamias as an alternative crop to sugarcane. Much of the once-lush island had been cleared for sugarcane. As

An Aborigine shells nuts to be used for cooking.

part of a Hawaiian reforestation project, he gathered seeds from Purvis's crop and raised eighteen thousand seedlings. Naquin planted the young trees in an orchard on the company's former sugar lands on Hawaii. Naquin promoted macadamias vigorously. Then his wife, Ethel, had the idea of dipping macadamias in chocolate. Her candies sold out fast at the local drugstore at Hilo, Hawaii, and soon were favorites across the Hawaiian Islands. During the Great Depression of the 1930s, many other parts of Honokaa's business slumped. The candy operation kept people in work. People made the nutty candy and created boxes in which to sell it. Between the 1930s and the 1960s, the macadamia orchard grew to thirty-six thousand trees on five hundred acres. It was not until the 1940s and 1950s that sales of Hawaiian macadamias became big outside of the islands.

Although Australia's first commercial plantation (large farm) was established in 1888 in New South Wales, the industry didn't take off right away. That changed in the 1960s when planters brought Hawaiian varieties to Queensland and New South Wales. Hawaiian breeders and growers had done sophisticated work with macadamias for many years. Australian growers with new plantations bought Hawaiian rootstock for a head start on growing macadamias. In fact, 90 percent of the macadamia trees cultivated in Australia come from Hawaiian cultivars.

Making Macadamias

Hawaii leads the world in macadamia production at 58 million pounds for 1998. Mauna Loa is the world's largest grower and processor of macadamia nuts, with ten thousand acres under cultivation. Australia gains ground each season. With a harvest of close to 50 million pounds, Australia supplies one-third of the world's production of macadamia nuts.

South Africa, Kenya, Brazil, Costa Rica,

It's a Fact!

Macadamia seeds, the gift of a sea captain to his brother in 1892, were planted on the island of Oahu. The nuts proved valuable years later in the 1930s, when the University of Hawaii sought macadamia seedlings for experimentation.

A high school student named Ralph Moltzav spent a summer vacation working at the Hawaii Agricultural Experiment Station. While there, Moltzav was the first person in North America to successfully graft macadamias.

Ten thousand acres of the island of Hawaii are devoted to growing macadamia nuts.

Guatemala, and California also boast substantial commercial macadamia orchards. The plant first arrived in California in 1877, when a tree grew on the campus of the University of California at Berkeley. It wasn't until about 1946 that people set up commercial orchards in California. These days, southern California grows about 2,500 acres of macadamias. Planters tend the trees in other favorable subtropical locales, too.

Cultivated macadamias grow from grafted trees created in nurseries. Workers move two-year-old trees from the nursery to open fields. Planters set the trees at intervals of twenty and twenty-five feet, in rows twenty-five to thirty feet apart. After about five more years, the trees begin to produce nuts. But the macadamia trees don't reach full production until they're about fifteen years old. That means farmers have to wait a long time to make a profit from new trees, so investing in macadamia orchards is costly.

Mechanical shakers can't help harvest macadamia nuts. Why? Because the macadamia tree's nuts don't all mature at one time—nuts become ripe and fall over the course of a few months. Shaking the trees would cause the immature nuts to fall along with the mature ones. Instead, many growers

At macadamia nut processing plants, workers inspect the dried nuts before packaging.

This horticulturist inspects a screen he designed to catch valuable macadamias.

It's a Fact!

The macadamia has many nicknames in English, including Queensland nuts, the Australian nut, Bauple nut, Bush nut, and Australian hazelnut.

let the nuts fall naturally to the ground, which is kept clear of debris. Once nuts hit the earth, harvesting begins. On large plantations, a worker may drive a mechanical harvester through the rows. The machine brushes the nuts onto a conveyor belt that carries them to bins. Some growers hire workers to gather fallen nuts by hand. In the fields or at a processing plant, machines use abrasive friction devices to rub the husks off the nutshells.

Growers may spread the husks over the ground as mulch.

Soon after they fall, macadamias are dried to reduce the chances of molding. The burning shells of previously processed macadamias fuel ovens in which the

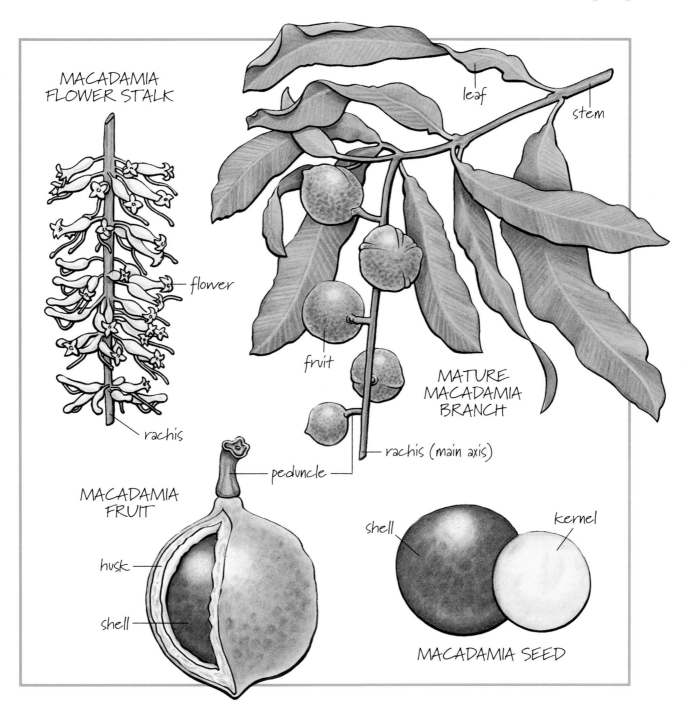

MACADAMIA
FLOWER STALK

leaf

stem

flower

rachis

fruit

MATURE
MACADAMIA
BRANCH

rachis (main axis)

peduncle

MACADAMIA
FRUIT

husk

shell

shell

kernel

MACADAMIA SEED

Macadamia nuts are processed *(left)* and packaged *(right)* then sent all over the world for people to enjoy.

nuts are dehydrated. As the nut dries, its kernel shrinks away from the shell. A kernel that's separated from the shell is less likely to be damaged when the very hard shell is cracked open. In fact, the macadamia is said to be the "the toughest nut to crack" of all edible nuts.

In the early era of the automobile in Hawaii, people spread the nuts on the ground, placed boards on top, and drove cars across to crush the shells. In modern times, two heavy rotating steel drums or rollers crack the macadamia shells. Another method employs a fixed sharp blade and a moving blade to slice open the shells.

Some Hawaiian packing companies roast the nuts in coconut oil before salting and packaging. Other methods include "dry roasting," or roasting without oil in a 350-degree oven. Macadamias are often vacuum packed in tins, jars, or foil packs before shipping. Macadamias packaged in bulk for use in commercial food processing may be whole, chopped, or ground.

Munching Macadamias

A few years ago, macadamia nuts started to appear in extravagant gourmet cookies made with white chocolate chips—a delicious alternative to the familiar walnut and chocolate chip variety! A Hawaiian classic of the past hundred years is called macadamia chiffon pie. Finely chopped macadamias lace the lemon-flavored filling, and the nuts even decorate the airy chiffon topping. Another rich pie treats macadamias like pecans when cooks mix the nuts with corn syrup and bake the blend in a pie shell.

Hawaiians use the macadamia chopped up in mango bread and in perfect pancakes slathered in coconut syrup. Chefs in Costa Rica, another macadamia country, prepare spicy nuts by cooking macadamias in oil flavored with a mixture of nutmeg, mace, cloves, and cinnamon. Costa Ricans also eat papaya bread with chopped macadamias and banana muffins filled with the nuts. In Australia's Queensland, chefs deep-fry a local fish called *barramundi* after dipping it in a chopped macadamia nut coating.

Macadamias can remain fresh for up to twelve months provided the right packaging materials are used.

A man selects nuts from large bins at a market in Istanbul, Turkey.

Dig In!

Fish with Macadamia Sauce (4 servings)

½ cup butter
¼ cup chopped macadamia nuts
4 fish fillets
Black pepper and paprika, to taste
1 tablespoon chopped fresh parsley
1 teaspoon fresh lemon juice
Pinch of fresh grated nutmeg.

Fish with macadamia sauce makes a healthy meal.

Australians love to combine macadamias with mild flavored fish. Try this sauce with sole or trout.

Over medium heat, melt the butter in a large heavy skillet or frying pan. Add the macadamia pieces and cook until the nuts turn golden brown. Take the nuts from the pan and set them aside. Place the fish fillets in the same pan (without washing it). Cook the fish over medium heat for two (if the fillets are thin) to four minutes (if the fillets are thick). Baste the fillets with butter as they cook. Sprinkle the fish with black pepper and paprika.

Remove the fillets from the pan and place them onto a platter. Return the nuts to the pan and add parsley, lemon juice, and nutmeg. Cook until the mixture is hot (less than two minutes) and pour it over the fish. Scrape the pan to get it all!

Glossary

cover crops: A crop planted to prevent soil from eroding (wearing away). Cover crops are plowed back into the ground to help keep the soil healthy.

cultivate: To foster the growth of a plant or animal by changing the conditions under which it grows in nature. A **cultivar** is a plant or animal created by cultivation.

domestication: Taming animals or adapting plants so they can safely live with or be eaten by humans.

grafting: To unite two plants by placing a stem or bud of one into a cut in the other, then allowing the two parts to grow together.

hybrid: The offspring of a pair of plants or animals of different varieties, species, or genera.

intercrop: To grow a variety of crops on the same piece of land, often by planting different crops in alternating rows.

kernel: The softer, inner part of a fruit stone, a seed, or a nut.

mission: A center where missionaries (religious teachers) work to spread their beliefs to other people and to teach a new way of life.

mulch: A protective ground cover. Mulch can be compost, paper, nutshells, or other materials. Mulch can help keep soil temperature constant, prevent soil from eroding, or control weeds.

photosynthesis: The chemical process by which green plants make energy-producing carbohydrates. The process involves the reaction of sunlight to carbon dioxide, water, and nutrients within plant tissues.

pollinate: The placement of pollen on a flower so that fruit will grow from the blossom. Bees pollinate the flowers of many plants.

staple food: A food plant that is widely cultivated across a given region and used on a regular basis.

tropics: The hot, wet zone around the earth's equator between the Tropic of Cancer and the Tropic of Capricorn.

Further Reading

Burns, Diane L. *Berries, Nuts and Seeds.* Minocqua, WI: NorthWord Press, 1996.

Earle, Olive L., and Michael Kantor. *Nuts.* New York: William Morrow and Co., 1975.

Fitzsimons, Cecilia. *Cereals, Nuts & Spices.* New York: Julian Messner, 1997.

George, Jean Craighead. *Acorn Pancakes, Dandelion Salad, and 38 Other Wild Recipes.* New York: HarperCollins Publishers, 1995.

Hughes, Meredith Sayles. *Tall and Tasty: Fruit Trees.* Minneapolis: Lerner Publications Company, 2000.

Inglis, Jane. *Fiber.* Minneapolis: Carolrhoda Books, Inc., 1993.

Root, Waverley. *Food.* New York: Simon and Schuster, 1980.

Tames, Richard. *Food: Feasts, Cooks, and Kitchens.* New York: Franklin Watts, 1994.

Trager, James. *The Food Chronology.* New York: Henry Holt and Company, 1995.

Shoppers gather around a nut seller at an open-air market in Manzini, Swaziland.

Index

About the Author

Meredith Sayles Hughes has been writing about food since the mid-1970s, when she and her husband, Tom Hughes, founded The Potato Museum in Brussels, Belgium. She has worked on two major exhibitions about food, one for the Smithsonian and one for the National Museum of Science and Technology in Ottawa, Ontario. Author of several articles on food history, Meredith has collaborated with Tom on a range of programs, lectures, workshops, and teacher-training sessions, as well as on *The Great Potato Book*. The Hugheses do exhibits and programs as The FOOD Museum in Albuquerque, New Mexico, where they live with their son, Gulliver.

Acknowledgments

For photographs and artwork: © Steve Brosnahan, p. 5; Tennessee State Museum Collection, detail of a painting by Carlyle Urello, p. 7; © David J. Forbert/AGStock USA, p. 11; Library of Congress, p. 12; © Richard T. Nowitz/Corbis, p. 16; John B. Sanfilippo and Son, Inc., pp. 17, 42; Agricultural Research Service, USDA, p. 18; © Lee Snider/Corbis, p. 19; © Robert Fried, pp. 20, 32; © September 8th Photography/Walt and Louiseann Pietrowicz, pp. 21, 37, 46 (top), 48 (left), 51, 53, 57 (bottom), 61, 65, 71 (bottom), 73, 84; NASA, p. 23; © Karen Su/Corbis, p. 25; © Ric Ergenbright/Corbis, p. 26 (top); © Bettmann/Corbis, pp. 26 (bottom), 30, 54 (bottom); © Erich Lessing/Art Resource, NY, p. 27; © William Dow/Corbis, p. 28; Goleta Valley Historical Society, p. 31; © Ed Young/AGStock USA, pp. 33, 35, 43; © Trip/A Ghazzal, p. 34; © Mark Garanger/Corbis, p. 36; © Maximilian Stock, Ltd./AGStock USA, p. 39; © Michael Busselle/Corbis, p. 40; Santa Barbara Mission Archive Library, p. 41; © David Thurber/AGStock USA, p. 42 (inset); © Stephanie Maze/Corbis, pp. 46 (bottom), 48 (right); © Jean-Leo Dugast/Panos Pictures, p. 47; © Dr. Roma Hoff, p. 49; © Daniel O'Leary/Panos Pictures, p. 50; © Eugene G. Schulz, p. 54 (top); © Patricia Ruben Miller/IPS, p. 55; © Trip/H. Rogers, pp. 57 (top), 60; California Pistachio Commission, p. 58; Minnesota Historical Society, p. 62; © Robert L. and Diane Wolfe, p. 63; © Sue Cunningham/SCP, p. 66; © Liba Taylor/Corbis, p. 67; © Holt Studios/Silvestre Silva, p. 68 (left); © Eric and David Hosking/Corbis, p. 68 (right); © Paul Seheult; Eye Ubiquitous/Corbis, pp. 70, 71 (top); © Charles O'Rear/Corbis, p. 72; © Dave Bartruff/ Corbis, p. 75; © Penny Tweedie/Corbis, p. 77; National Archives, pp. 79 (top), 80; Mauna Loa Macadamia Nut Corporation, pp. 79 (bottom), 82 (right); © James L. Amos/Corbis, p. 82 (left); © Trip/J. Greenberg, p. 83; © Trip/J. Denham, p. 86. Sidebar and back cover artwork by John Erste. All other artwork by Laura Westlund. Cover photo by Jim Simondet.
For quoted material: p. 4, M.F.K. Fisher, *The Art of Eating* (New York: MacMillan Reference, 1990); p. 10, Eugene Walter, *American Cooking* (Alexandria, Virginia: Time-Life Books, 1971); p. 24, Rhoda Thomas Tripp, *International Thesaurus of Quotations* (New York: Harper & Row, 1970); p. 38, Troth Wells, *The World in Your Kitchen* (Freedom, California: The Crossing Press, 1993); p. 52, Waverley Root, *Food* (New York: Simon & Schuster, 1980); p. 64, March Egerton, *Since Eve Ate Apples* (Portland, Oregon: Tsunami Press, 1994); p. 74, Suncoast Macadamias, (Queensland, Australia: <http://www.goldmacs.com.au>)
For recipes (some slightly adapted for kids): pp. 27, 37, Meredith Sayles Hughes; pp. 51, 73 reprinted with permission from *The World in Your Kitchen* by Troth Wells. © 1993. Published by *The Crossing Press*: Freedom, California; p. 61, printed with the permission of the California Pistachio Commission; p. 84, as quoted by Suncoast Macadamias, (Queensland, Australia: <http://www.goldmacs.com.au>).